You Are More Than Enough

You Are More Than Enough

A Children's Book on Self-Love and Compassion

Written by Julie Brown

You Are More Than Enough – A Children's Book on Self–Love and Compassion

Published by Gatekeeper Press
7853 Gunn Hwy., Suite 209
Tampa, FL 33626
www.GatekeeperPress.com

Library of Congress Control Number: 2024930134

ISBN (hardcover): 9781662945915
ISBN (paperback): 9781662945922
eISBN: 9781662945939

Dedicated to Allianna Joy, my angel.
You are the light of my life.

When your voice starts to quiver
and your hands start to shake—
You're enough.
You're enough.
You're enough, it will say.

In your skin and your bones
and your perfect, sweet face—
You're enough.
You're enough.
You're enough, it will say.

When the world seems too scary,
when you think you can't stand—
Take a deep breath.
Hold on to my hand.

I'm the friend deep inside you,
the voice always here.
I see you.
I love you.
I am you, my dear.

Sometimes you can't hear me.
Sometimes you'll feel weak.
But if you get quiet and still,
you'll hear me speak.

You can do what your heart wants.
Follow it without fear.
Reach for your wishes;
they're already here.

I'm the wind in your hair.
I'm the beat in your chest.
I'm the smile on your face,
and I'm always impressed.

No matter what happens,
and no matter how scared,
you can do it, for certain!
You're always prepared.

So, follow your heart.
Raise your head up high.
You are worthy of everything,
no matter how high.

You can do it! Don't give up!
You've got everything that you need.
Don't wait, but don't hurry.
Let your heart take the lead.

There is no upper limit,
no thing you can't reach.
You are great.
You are whole.
Just how you are, you're complete.

The End

Who is this voice? This is the voice you can hear when you open your heart and become quiet and still. It's the true you—the heart, not the mind. So many times we hear an inner critic of doubt, worry, and fear. We're often paralyzed by this voice that limits the potential of all that we are and everything we truly want to be.

ABOUT THE AUTHOR

Julie Brown is a children's book author currently residing in Northern California. She is also a nurse who specializes in pediatrics (children) and mother. Julie's calling, both professionally and personally, has long been to encourage self-love in others, but specifically children as she works daily with kids who are battling various medical challenges. The inspiration for this book came from those patients, as well as her daughter, Allianna, who lives with cystic fibrosis, a rare and progressive lung disease that currently has no cure. Although her hope is to inspire self-love in others, it has been a lifelong struggle of hers to overcome her own personal challenges with depression and anxiety. Julie believes that in being authentic and vulnerable, she creates a much needed space for others to do the same. Bearing witness to several friends, family members, and colleagues who struggle with mental health, it is Julie's dream to create a world with less bias where people of all kinds are able to speak their truth without fear of rejection and stigma that so often comes with mental illness.